I0528710

Power Tools Part 3: Holy Spirit Power

Building Foundations: A Spirit Filled Children's Church Curriculum

Pastor Tamera Kraft
Revival Fire 4 Kids Resource

Mt Zion Ridge Press
http://mtzionridgepress.com
Managing Editors: Michelle L. Levigne and Tamera Lynn Kraft
Cover Art: Tamera Lynn Kraft

ISBN: 978-1-955838-12-2

Registration and Digital Files (Available for FREE with purchase of the curriculum): Digital files (jpeg graphics, video clips, other resources) are available to anyone who purchases and registers this curriculum at no additional cost. To register, click on this link http://eepurl.com/glsELH or type it in the address box on your browser and fill out the form. We never sell or give away any information we receive.

DVD: If you prefer a DVD of Jpeg images and video clips, you may purchase it at http://mtzionridgepress.com for an additional cost.

Power Tools is a 3 part curriculum which includes these sections that can be bought together in one manual or bought separately:

- Part 1 – Prayer Power (4 lessons on the power of prayer included in this manual)
- Part 2 – Worship Power (4 Lessons on the power of worshipping God)
- **Part 3 – Holy Spirit Power (5 lessons on how the baptism and gifts of the Holy Spirit equip you with power)**

Power Tools is available in PDF download and print. Each part of *Power Tools* is available separately in PDF download or print.

All Scripture in this curriculum is from the NIV (2011) Bible unless otherwise designated.

THE HOLY BIBLE, NEW INTERNATIONAL VERSION®, NIV® Copyright © 1973, 1978, 1984, 2011 by Biblica, Inc.® Used by permission. All rights reserved worldwide.

Some Scripture is also used from these versions:

THE HOLY BIBLE, INTERNATIONAL CHILDREN'S BIBLE® ICB Copyright© 1986, 1988, 1999, 2015 by Tommy Nelson™, a division of Thomas Nelson. Thomas Nelson is a registered trademark of HarperCollins Christian Publishing, Inc.

NEW KING JAMES VERSION® NKJV® Scripture taken from the New King James Version®. Copyright © 1982 by Thomas Nelson. Used by permission. All rights reserved.

Power Tools © Mt Zion Ridge Press, 2021. All rights reserved.

Copyright permissions for this curriculum: When you register this curriculum, you are granted permission to make as many copies as needed for the use of the church or ministry registered only. ***Do not distribute this material to other churches or ministries without permission. Copying materials in any other way violates copyright laws.***

For questions about copyright issues or other matter concerning rights for this curriculum, contact revivalfire4kids@att.net.

Building Foundations Curriculum is a Revival Fire for Kids resource. For more information about Revival Fire for Kids, check out their website at http://revivalfire4kids.net

Materials included:

Holy Spirit Power: 5 complete downloadable lessons including 10 object lessons, 10 skits, 10 games, 5 Bible Stories, 5 memory verse activities, graphics to be used in PowerPoint slides for 5 lessons, 5 small group

discussions or activities, and optional lessons and activities. Lessons, graphics, videos, and Family Devotion Handouts will be available for immediate download upon registering this curriculum at this link: http://eepurl.com/glsELH.

Table of Contents

How To Use This Curriculum:

Scriptural Premise: God does not leave us powerless in our Christian journey. He gives us tools to empower us for everything He wants us to do. Among these power tools are prayer, worship, the baptism of the Holy Spirit, and the gifts of the Holy Spirit.

Decorations: Decorations and set design should reflect building construction with drills, saws, and power tools. If you have purchased *The Journey*, another *Building Foundations Curriculum*, you could use the decorations for *The Journey* and add power tools. You could also borrow power tools from someone and set up a power tools garage or store.

Another idea is to use a backdrop with the cover picture of *Power Tools or Power Tools* backdrop as templates for a backdrop. You can use any image included with this curriculum by projecting the image using a video projector onto a box or backdrop and drawing it. Use your creativity.

Italics: Italics are used for Scripture. They are also used in this curriculum for passages or speeches the teacher or worker may want to say in their own words. For skits, italics are only used to designate the person speaking.

Welcome:

Welcome: Each lesson will welcome the children with an introduction to that day's message.

Prayer: It's important to start each lesson with prayer.

Rules: A list of 5 Ups are included in the graphics available after registration. Rehearse the rules every week.

Theme Song: Get the kids up and moving at the beginning of every lesson with a fun theme song. Theme song that will work with this curriculum are *Rest on Us* by Maverick City Music, *Power (Acts 1:8 ESV)* by Seeds Family Worship, or *Waymaker* by Leeland.

Memory Verse: Every lesson has a memory verse. The verse will be included in a slide and will be illustrated in three ways. You can choose to use any of these illustrations to teach the verse, or you could use all three throughout your lesson.

Memory Verse Skit: A puppet or live skit with Doctor Word is included in each lesson to introduce the Memory Verse. The person doing the skit can dress as a doctor or in scrubs. If a doctor, nurse, or medical professional attends you church, it would be great to him for your skits and have him wear his work clothes. You can also use a doctor puppet for these skits if you have a puppet team.

Memory Verse Talk: This is a short talk explaining what the verse means to the children. Memorizing God's Word is important, but it's more important for your students to know what a verse means.

Memory Verse Activity: Children learn by seeing, reading, hearing, and doing. The memory verse activity is a simple tool to help students remember the verse.

Game Time: A Game Time slide is included with registration for this curriculum. It isn't necessary to include a game with every week's lesson, but if you do, you should have a fun game that relates to the lessons. Game Time is the place for that. You may also want to save the game for last so, if the adult service runs long, you can play games until the parents arrive to retrieve their children.

Video Clips: *Power Tools Countdown* and video clips for some lessons are included with *Holy Spirit Power* along with other downloadable files. A link to a Dropbox files with be sent to your email after you have registered your curriculum. *Building Foundations* doesn't provide video curriculum to teach the lessons. Instead, it provides short, fun video clips to help the children remember the lesson in a fun way.

Offering: Lessons include a short talk on why children should give in the offering. You can expand the fun by having an offering contest with the boys against the girls. You can use a scale with buckets or have two offering plates and count the money. Once a month or once a quarter, have a special reward for the winning team.

Praise & Worship: Each week, a time of praise and worship is included to ready the students' hearts to hear the Word of God. This curriculum does not provide music because every church has different musical needs.

Lesson of the Week:

Skit: Two skits about each week's lesson are included. One skit uses a doctor, Doctor Word, to introduce the memory verse for the day. Another skit uses a silly character named Tyler the Power Tool Guy or Gal. These skits require few props and only two people, the leader and another worker, making them easy for even small churches to use. Doctor Word skits can be used as puppet skits if you have a puppet ministry. Tyler the Power Tool Guy or Gal could also be used with puppets but may need some modification when props are involved.

Bible Story: Each week, a Bible story is included to go with the lesson.

Object Lessons: At least two object lessons illustrate the points of each week's lesson. Resources for the object lessons are not included.

Message: A short message ties up the lesson for the day and asks for a response from the students.

Optional Resources: Optional Resources are included in some lessons with object lessons and other interactive events as suggestions for additional teaching activities. The props for optional resources are not included but are easy to obtain.

Small Group Chat/Activity: Some children's ministries prefer to end each children's service with a small group chat, or they have a small group Bible study at some time during the week. Small group chat questions and activities are included for these purposes. Divide students into small groups of not more than six children. You can divide them by ages or include different ages together. Questions and instructions for activities are included to help the leader facilitate a chat with the students about the lesson. Small group sessions will help your students go home with practical applications for what they have learned.

Home Application: Each lesson will include a handout for the children to take home. Each handout will include this week's memory verse, a summary of the lesson, a Bible reading for each day, and a weekly family activity. This handout is available as a printable PDF download upon registration of this curriculum. This will be helpful guide for parents who have family devotions.

Registration and Digital Files (Available for FREE with purchase of the curriculum): Digital files (jpeg graphics, video clips, other resources) are available to anyone who purchases and registers this curriculum at no additional cost. To register, click on this link http://eepurl.com/glsELH or type it in the address box on your browser and fill out the form. We never sell or give away any information we receive.

Power Tools 3: Holy Spirit Power Lessons

The Holy Spirit Baptism

Acts 2:4 (NIV) *All of them were filled with the Holy Spirit and began to speak in other tongues as the Spirit enabled them.*

The Holy Spirit Makes Us Bold

Acts 1:8 (NIV) *But you shall receive power when the Holy Spirit has come upon you; and you shall be witnesses to Me in Jerusalem, and in all Judea and Samaria, and to the end of the earth.*

The Holy Spirit Helps Us

John 14:16 (NKJV) *And I will pray the Father, and He will give you another Helper, that He may abide with you forever.*

The Holy Spirit Reveals Things

Acts 2:17 (NIV) *"In the last days," God says, "I will pour out my Spirit on all people. Your sons and daughters will prophesy, your young men will see visions, your old men will dream dreams."*

The Holy Spirit Gives Us His Power

Zechariah 4:6b (NIV) *"Not by might nor by power, but by my Spirit," says the Lord Almighty.*

Lesson 1 - The Holy Spirit Baptism

Focus Point: Jesus wants to baptize us in the Holy Spirit

Goal: Students will learn who the Holy Spirit is, what the baptism of the Holy Spirit is, and will be encouraged to experience it for themselves.

Verse of the Day: Acts 2:4 (NIV) *All of them were filled with the Holy Spirit and began to speak in other tongues as the Spirit enabled them.*

Supplies Needed:

- doctor puppet or doctor costume for skit
- portable toolbox with various tools
- Tyler the Power Tool Guy Skit: Tyler wears a portable toolbox or toolbelt with various tools and is dressed in blue jeans and a plaid shirt, etc.
- drill or another power tool
- glass of water
- bowls of water
- small cups
- spoons
- 23 small round balloons
- magic markers
- packing tape
- pin or needle
- electric fan
- pictures of fire for each of your students and one for teacher (found in downloadable resources)
- adult headband
- clear drinking glass
- pitcher
- tiny doll or action figure that will fit in the drinking glass
- tray to catch excess water
- pitcher of water
- 5 paper or Styrofoam cups
- milk (optional)
- chocolate syrup (optional)
- spoon (optional)
- one piece of candy for each student

Opening: *Power Tools Countdown* or *Power Tools* Slide (Available free with registration of this curriculum.)

Welcome: The Holy Spirit

Supplies needed: glass of water

Welcome to Holy Spirit Power. For the next few weeks, we will learn about one of the most powerful tools in a Christian's life, the power of the Holy Spirit. God is one God but three parts. It's hard for even theologians to understand, but it's sort of like this glass of water. This is water also known as H2O. But if I were to heat this water to boiling, it would turn into steam. Yet, even though it's steam, it would still be H2O. If I were to freeze this water, it would turn into ice. But it would still be H2O. God the Father is God. God the Son is God. And God the Holy Spirit is God. They have different functions and personalities, but they are the same. They are one God just as this glass of water can become steam or ice is the same H2O.

You've probably already heard a lot about our Heavenly Father, God the Father. I'm sure you've heard a lot about God the Son, Jesus. For the next few weeks, we're going to learn more about God the Holy Spirit.

Prayer: Ask a child to pray over the service.

Rules: (use rules slide) Go over 5 Up rules.

Go over the *5 Ups Rules*: 1. Sit up straight. 2. Listen up. 3. Hush up. 4. Don't get up and run around or go to the bathroom. 5. Worship Up! (stand up and participate during praise and worship)

Theme or Activity Songs: Choose one of two fast moving activity or theme songs that go with the curriculum.

Game Time: Minute to Win It - Fill the cup (use game time slide)

Supplies Needed: bowls of water, small cups, spoons (You will need one set for each student participating in the game.)

This is a Minute to Win It Game, so you can use a minute countdown or a phone timer. Choose 2-4 students to participate. The goal of the game is to fill the cup with water. Using only a spoon, transfer the water from the bowl to the cup. If nobody manages to fill their cup by the time the minute is up, the student with the fullest cup wins.

I'm glad it's so much easier for the Holy Spirit to fill us than it is to fill these cups with water using only a spoon.

Memory Verse Skit: (use Holy Spirit Power Lesson 1, slide A)

Supplies needed: doctor puppet or doctor costume for skit

Doctor Word: Hi kids. I'm Doctor Word. I'm called that because I'm a doctor and because I love the Word of God. Many times, I have a patient who doesn't have insurance and can't afford the medicine prescribed to help his ailment. When that happens, I try to find medicine I can give him for free. Sometimes I'll have a sample the drug companies gave me, and I'll use those samples to give to these patients.

I'm glad none of us have to pay for the baptism of the Holy Spirit or work really hard to get it. The baptism of the Holy Spirit is a free gift to God's children when they seek Him. Our memory verse today talks about when the disciples in the Bible were first filled with the Holy Spirit.

Acts 2:4 (NIV) *All of them were filled with the Holy Spirit and began to speak in other tongues as the Spirit enabled them.*

Offering: Freely Give

Matthew 10:8 (NIV) says, "Freely you have received; freely give." What that means is because God has given us so much, including the baptism of the Holy Spirit, we shouldn't have a problem with freely giving in the offering.

Skit: Tyler the Power Tool Guy Renovates a House

Supplies Needed: Tyler has a portable toolbox or toolbelt with various tools and is dressed in blue jeans and a plaid shirt, etc., drill or another power tool. If you use a girl in the skit, have her dress the same and call her Tyler the Power Tool Gal.

(Tyler, the Power Tool Guy, comes into the room with a power tool. It doesn't matter which tool, but it should make noise when you start it up. A drill would work well.)

Leader: Hello, Power Tool Guy. So, how are you doing?

Tyler the Power Tool Guy: I'm doing great. I'm so excited. I can hardly wait.

Leader: I'm glad you're doing so great. What are you excited about?

Tyler: I just got the best job I've ever had.

Leader: That's wonderful. Does it pay better than the other jobs?

Tyler: Not really. The pay is about the same, but it has other perks.

Leader: That's great. I can see you're happy about it. What is this wonderful job?

Tyler: I get to renovate an old house.

Leader: Okay. What's so great about that job?

Tyler: Are you kidding? I get to tear down walls and cabinets and destroy things before I start putting in new stuff.

Leader: I'm happy for you. It sounds like fun.

Tyler: It is, but that's not all. I get to use almost all of my power tools on this job. (Starts power tool and revs it so it makes a lot of noise.) I feel so powerful.

Leader: That's awesome, Tyler. Today, we're talking about how to be powerful in our Christian lives.

Tyler: Do you get to tear things down and use power tools?

Leader: Not exactly. We get power through the baptism of the Holy Spirit.

Tyler: That's awesome. My power tools cost a lot of money. Do you have to pay anything or do anything to get Holy Spirit power.

Leader: Not a thing. The Holy Spirit comes to live inside of us when we get saved, and the baptism of the Holy Spirit is absolutely free for believers.

Tyler: Wow, that's amazing. I have to go make my plans for renovating the house now. Bye.

(Exits)

Verse of the Day: Acts 2:4 (NIV) *All of them were filled with the Holy Spirit and began to speak in other tongues as the Spirit enabled them.*

Memory Verse Talk: Filled with the Holy Spirit (use Holy Spirit Power Lesson 1, slide A)

Supplies needed: balloon

Speaking in tongues means speaking in a language we don't know. God gives us the words to speak when we are baptized in the Holy Spirit.

Have you ever wondered why people who are filled with the Holy Spirit speak in tongues? I used to wonder that until a minister told me that it's harder to control our words than any other part of the body. I believe that's true. When we become so yielded to the Holy Spirit that He controls what we say, even what language we say it in, that means we have allowed the Jesus to baptize in the Holy Spirit. We have given control of our tongues and our words to the Holy Spirit.

Blow up a balloon. *When I hold this blown-up balloon, I control it. I can move it anywhere I want. I can move it up, or I can move it down. But if I allow the balloon to have control, I don't know what this balloon is going to do.*

Let go of the balloon and let it fly off as the air escapes. *When I release my control, the Holy Spirit will do what He wants in my life just as the balloon does what it wants.*

The disciples in the Bible did just that. They let go of their control, and they allowed the Holy Spirit to control them. That's when they were filled and began to speak in other tongues.

Memory Verse Activity: Balloon Pop

Supplies needed: 22 balloons, magic markers, packing tape, pin or needle

Preparation: Blow up 22 balloons. Use the marker to write each word of the memory verse on a separate balloon. The address is also written on a balloon. Tape the balloons to the wall in order of the memory verse.

Warn the students ahead of time you are going to pop the balloons in case any of them are startled by the sound. Some may need to leave the room until you are done. Have students repeat the memory verse several times. As you pop each balloon, have the students say the memory verse again until there are no more balloons to pop.

Bible Story: The Upper Room

(Acts 2)

Supplies needed: powerful electric fan, headband with picture of fire taped onto it (picture found in downloadable resources)

Preparation: Choose 2-4 students to make fun and say, "You're drunk," at the appropriate time. Let the other students know to tell each other, "That's amazing," at the appropriate time.

Read the account in Acts 2 with the following instructions.

Acts 2:1 When the day of Pentecost came, they were all together in one place.

Acts 2:2 Suddenly a sound like the blowing of a violent wind came from heaven and filled the whole house where they were sitting. Turn on fan and blow it toward the students.

Acts 2:3 They saw what seemed to be tongues of fire that separated and came to rest on each of them. Place the fire headband with picture of fire on your head.

Acts 2:4 All of them were filled with the Holy Spirit and began to speak in other tongues as the Spirit enabled them. Explain to your students that speaking in tongues is speaking a language they don't know.

Acts 2:5-8, 11-12 Now there were staying in Jerusalem God-fearing Jews from every nation under heaven. When they heard this sound, a crowd came together in bewilderment, because each one heard their own language being spoken. Utterly amazed, they asked: "Aren't all these who are speaking Galileans? Then how is it that each of us hears them in our native language? ...we hear them declaring the wonders of God in our own tongues!" Amazed and perplexed, they asked one another, "What does this mean?" Have your students shrug their shoulders and say, "What could this mean to one another?"

Acts 2:13 Some, however, made fun of them and said, "They have had too much wine." Have the students you assigned to say, "You're drunk."

After this, Peter stood and addressed the crowd. He told them it was too early to be drunk, but this was prophesied in the Book of Joel. Then he spoke about how Jesus died and rose again to save them from their sins. The people asked Peter what they needed to do to be saved. Peter told them in verses 38-39.

Acts 2:38-39 Peter replied, "Repent and be baptized, every one of you, in the name of Jesus Christ for the forgiveness of your sins. And you will receive the gift of the Holy Spirit. The promise is for you and your children and for all who are far off—for all whom the Lord our God will call."

The baptism of the Holy Spirit was for them, but it's also for anyone who is a Christian – including children. Including each of you.

Praise and Worship: Choose a couple of fast song and a slow song to lead children into praise and worship. It works well to talk to the children about what worship is and why it's important before you enter into this time. You can have a children's praise team, but until they understand leading praise and worship, have an adult leader or yourself be the worship leader.

Video: Tongues or Shoes (available through downloadable resources)

Object Lessons:

1. 3 Baptisms

Supplies needed: clear glass, pitcher, tiny doll or action figure that will fit in a glass, tray to catch excess water

Sometimes we hear about baptism, and we think there is only one kind of baptism. That is when you go into the baptism pool and the pastor dunks you, but there are many types of baptism in your Christian life. I'm going to show you the three main baptisms available to every Christian.

When you are saved, the Holy Spirit comes to live inside you. Pour water into the glass. *When He does this, you become a Christian and are baptized into the body of Christ.*

Then there is baptism in water. After you become a Christian, at some point, you are baptized in water. That shows to everyone that you made a commitment to give your life to Christ. It doesn't make you a Christian, but it shows you are a Christian. Hold the doll above the water. *When you are baptized, you are showing that Christ died for your sins,* Dunk the doll in the glass of water above its head. *Christ was buried.* Raise the doll back out of the water. *Then Christ rose again defeating sin and death.*

Have a helper or a child demonstrate what would happen to someone baptized in water at your church. Emphasize that the child would be warned and have time to hold his breath, and the pastor wouldn't keep him under the water for more than a couple of seconds. Have your students hold their breaths for ten seconds to show how they can all hold their breaths longer than they would need to during the baptism. Answer any questions they might have about water baptism. Encourage your students to get baptized at the next opportunity the church gives. You may want to discuss this with your pastor so he can schedule a baptism.

As you say this next part, continue to pour water in the cup until it overflows. *There are many other baptisms. There's a baptism of fire, a baptism of peace, a baptism of joy, and others. God fills us often if we allow Him too. Then there is the baptism of the Holy Spirit. This happens when you are completely yielded to the Holy Spirit.* Hold up the glass of water. *It's like taking this glass of water and throwing it into the middle of the ocean. You won't know where the water in the glass starts or ends. It will be a part of the ocean. That's the baptism of the Holy Spirit. The first evidence that you've received the baptism of the Holy Spirit is when you begin to speak in other languages or tongue. Sometimes it will be gibberish at first, just as a baby talks gibberish when he's learning to talk, but as you continue to be filled, your prayer language will grow.*

2. Who Can Receive the Baptism of the Holy Spirit?

Supplies needed: pitcher of water, 5 paper or Styrofoam cups, tray or bowl to catch excess water

Preparation: First cup is turned upside down. Second cup has dirt, trash, and mud in it. Third cup has holes in the bottom. Fourth cup is cut in half length wise with the cup side turned toward the children. Fifth cup is right side up and has nothing in it.

Even though the Baptism of the Holy Spirit is a free gift that God wants to give His children, there are ways to prepare to receive this free gift.

Pour water on the first cup. *This represents a child who has not asked Jesus Christ into His heart. Since he doesn't know Christ as his Savior, he can't receive the baptism of the Holy Spirit.*

Show your students the inside of the second cup. *This child can't receive the baptism of the Holy Spirit because he has sin in his life. He needs to confess his sin to God and ask God to forgive him before he receives the baptism of the Holy Spirit.*

Pour water in the third cup. *This child is saved and has been forgiven of his sin, but he can't receive the baptism of the Holy Spirit because he doesn't have faith that God will fill Him. Maybe he thinks he's too young or not good enough. Or maybe he believes that God only wants to fill people like the preacher and the children's pastor. He needs to plug the holes in his faith. The way to do that is learn about the Holy Spirit from the Bible, then seek the Holy Spirit. Before long, those faith holes will be plugged up.*

Pour water in the fourth cup. *This child can't receive the Holy Spirit because he hasn't surrendered himself completely to God. We all spend a lifetime giving ourselves to God. It will never be complete, but to receive the baptism of the Holy Spirit, we need to be open to God and commit our lives to Him. We need to be thirsty for more of Him.*

Pour water into the fifth cup until it overflows. *God wants to fill you with the baptism of the Holy Spirit.*

Lead the students in a prayer that addresses each of the children represented by the different cups.

Optional Object Lesson: Stir Up the Holy Spirit

Supplies needed: glass, milk, chocolate syrup, spoon

Pour milk in the glass. *The milk represents us. When we get saved, the Holy Spirit comes to live inside of us.* Pour chocolate syrup in milk. *Even though this milk has the chocolate in it, the chocolate has not taken over every part of the milk. When we are saved, the Holy Spirit comes to live inside of us. He guides us, comforts us, and shows us when we sin and need to ask God's forgiveness, but we aren't fully taken over by the Holy Spirit. We need to stir up the gift of the Holy Spirit within us.*

Stir the chocolate milk. *As I stir this milk, the chocolate seeps into every part of it. You can't say this part is chocolate and this part is milk because it is all chocolate milk. That's the way it is when we stir up the Holy Spirit inside of us, and He baptizes us in the Holy Spirit.*

Now, what happens if we set the chocolate milk in the refrigerator and leave it for a few days. Allow the students to answer. *The milk and the chocolate separate. You begin to see what part is milk and what part is chocolate. That's why it is important to continue to stir up the gift and keep being filled with the Holy Spirit.* Take a drink of the milk. *Hmm. Taste and see that the Lord is good.*

Message: How to Receive the Free Gift

Supplies needed: one piece of candy for each student

Give each student a piece of candy. Unless your church's guidelines don't permit it, allow your students to eat the candy while you're talking.

Have someone in your church give a testimony about being baptized in the Holy Spirit as a child. If you have children in your ministry who were baptized in the Holy Spirit, have them talk about their experience. If you were baptized in the Holy Spirit as a child, you may also want to give your testimony.

Ask the students what they had to do to receive the candy they're eating. They may answer that they didn't have to do anything, or they had to reach out and grab it. Tell the children that the baptism of the Holy Spirit is a free gift they only need to reach out and grab it.

In a moment, we're going to take some time to worship God and allow His Holy Spirit to move. Some of you may not be ready to receive the baptism of the Holy Spirit yet, and that's okay. You can take your time and learn more before you decide, but you can still spend time worshipping and seeking God today. The Holy Spirit may decide to baptize you with His joy or His peace today. We're going to believe that God will baptize those who want it with the Holy Spirit. Here's how you can grab hold of the baptism of the Holy Spirit just as you grabbed hold of the free candy.

1. Ask Jesus for the baptism of the Holy Spirit. Once you've asked Jesus to baptize you in the Holy Spirit, He will do it. Even if it doesn't happen right away, God will fulfill His promises. Let's take a moment to pray and ask Jesus to baptize us in the Holy Spirit.

2. Praise God out loud using your voices. God doesn't zap you against your will to get you to speak in tongues. God uses your voices, but it is Him speaking through you. Use your voices to praise God out loud, and let Him do the rest. That doesn't mean you have to shout, but you can. As long as you speak loud enough for you to hear yourself, He can fill you. You might want to say things like, "Hallelujah. I love you, Jesus. I want more of you, Holy Spirit. Praise you, Lord."

3. Surrender your words. When you start to feel your tongues and mouths forming in strange ways, surrender your words to God and allow Him to speak through you.

4. Wait on God. Sometimes you aren't baptized in the Holy Spirit right away. God wants to fill you. Keep seeking Him and praising him, and it will happen. Sometimes, it's hard to concentrate on God when all these people are around, but you don't have to be in church to be baptized in the Holy Spirit. It might happen today while you're at home or tonight while you're in your bed praising God.

Response Time:

Encourage the children to come to the front to worship God. You may want to ask the children seeking the baptism of the Holy Spirit to stand in one area. Play worship music and encourage all the children to worship God using their voices. When you see God moving on certain children, lay your hand gently on their heads. Don't pray loudly over them because you might distract them. Allow the Holy Spirit to do the work. Instruct them only if you feel led by the Holy Spirit to do so.

After the response time, ask the students if any of them were baptized in the Holy Spirit. Encourage them to continue to seek the Holy Spirit and learn more about Him.

Small Group Activity: Fire Headband Craft

Supplies needed: child's headband or yarn for each student, fire picture for each student (found in downloadable resources), tape, scissors

Have each student cut out the fire picture, then tape it to their headbands or yarn they will tie around their heads. Now they have a reminder to wear about being baptized in the Holy Spirit. While the students are doing the craft, ask them if they have any questions about the baptism of the Holy Spirit. Tell them about your experiences with the Holy Spirit.

Lesson 2 – The Holy Spirit Makes Us Bold

Focus Point: The Holy Spirit makes us bold.

Goal: The students will learn being filled with the Holy Spirit will give them the boldness they need to share the Gospel.

Verse of the Day: Acts 1:8 (NIV) *But you shall receive power when the Holy Spirit has come upon you; and you shall be witnesses to Me in Jerusalem, and in all Judea and Samaria, and to the end of the earth.*

Supplies Needed:

- doctor puppet or doctor costume for skit
- portable toolbox with various tools
- Tyler the Power Tool Guy Skit: Tyler wears a portable toolbox or toolbelt with various tools and is dressed in blue jeans and a plaid shirt, etc.
- sledge hammer or chain saw
- plastic eggs
- strips of paper
- rubber chicken
- rubber boat or toy that floats
- clear small bowl filled halfway with water
- pitcher of water
- tray to catch excess water
- flashlight
- batteries
- Steve Spangler Science Energy Stick (optional)

Opening: *Power Tools Countdown* (optional) or *Power Tools* Slide

Welcome: Be Bold

Welcome children. Today, we're going to learn about being bold in the power of the Holy Spirit. One definition of bold is to be fearless in the face of danger. Many of the early church leaders had that kind of boldness. Missionaries who go to foreign lands also have that kind of boldness. All of us need that boldness in our every day lives. We need that boldness in our homes, our schools, and in our neighborhoods so we can share the Gospel of Christ and live a Christian life that pleases God. Even if you are naturally shy, the Holy Spirit will give you the boldness you need.

Prayer: Ask a child to pray over the service.

Rules: (use rules slide) Go over the 5 Ups Rules.

Go over the *5 Ups Rules*: 1. Sit up straight. 2. Listen up. 3. Hush up. 4. Don't get up and run around or go to the bathroom. 5. Worship Up! (stand up and participate during praise and worship)

Theme or Activity Songs: Choose one of two fast moving activity or theme songs that go with the curriculum.

Game Time: Chicken, Chicken, Rooster (use game time slide)

Supplies needed: none

Play this game like Duck, Duck, Goose, but have the students say, *Chicken, Chicken, Rooster* instead. This is normally a pre-school game, but have fun with it.

Have the students sit in a circle. The student who is it goes around the circle and taps each child saying, "Chicken." When a student is tapped and the person who is it says, "Rooster," the tapped student must run after the student who is it and tap that person before he sits in the place of the student who was tapped. If the tapped student fails, he's it. Play several times.

The student who was tapped had to show boldness chasing the student who was it. The Holy Spirit wants to take the chicken out of us and give us boldness when we tell others about Jesus.

Memory Verse Skit: (use Holy Spirit Power Lesson 2, slide A)

Supplies needed: doctor puppet or doctor costume for skit

Doctor Word: Hi kids. I'm Doctor Word. I'm called that because I'm a doctor and because I love the Word of God. When I first became a doctor, I was always worried I might make a mistake. In most professions, people make mistakes, and it doesn't matter that much. But when a doctor makes a mistake, it can have life-threatening consequences. Because I was so afraid of making a mistake, sometimes I didn't diagnose illnesses right away. This caused problems for my patients. I didn't know how to fix my problem, so I prayed about it. Jesus filled me with the Holy Spirit, and things changed. The Holy Spirit gave me boldness to treat patients in the right way. I became a better doctor. Because of this, I was able to go on mission's trips to other countries. I would treat their illnesses and share the Gospel of Jesus Christ with them. That's why today's memory verse is so important. Acts 1:8 (NIV) says, "*But you shall receive power when the Holy Spirit has come upon you; and you shall be witnesses to Me in Jerusalem, and in all Judea and Samaria, and to the end of the earth.*" One type of power the Holy Spirit gives us is boldness. I'm so glad He gave me the boldness I needed.

Offering: Giving Boldly

2 Corinthians 3:12 (NIV) says, "Therefore, since we have such a hope, we are very bold." In other words, because Christ gives us hope, and because we have the Holy Spirit inside of us, we can do everything with boldness. We can even give in the offering with boldness. Let's give boldly today.

If you have a mission's project your church supports, this would be a great time to tell your students about the bold missionaries and take a mission's offering.

Have a child pray over the offering.

Skit: Tyler the Power Tool Guy Boldly Demolishes

Supplies needed: sledge hammer or chain saw. Tyler has a portable toolbox or toolbelt with various tools and is dressed in blue jeans and a plaid shirt, etc. If you use a girl in the skit, have her dress the same and call her Tyler the Power Tool Gal.

Tyler the Power Tool Guy: (Comes in whistling or humming)

Leader: You sound happy, Tyler. Did you start on your job remodeling that house?

Tyler: I sure did, and I'm using tools like this to demolish walls and cabinets I no longer need.

Leader: So, you like to demolish houses.

Tyler: I didn't at first, but now I love it.

Leader: Why didn't you like it at first?

Tyler: It took me forever to tear down a wall or rip out a cabinet, but now I know the secret to get it done faster.

Leader: Really? What secret is that?

Tyler: I was using this tool too timidly like I might break something. I learned I have to demolish with boldness and power, or I won't be effective.

Leader: That's interesting. Today, we're learning how the Holy Spirit gives us boldness to tell others about Jesus.

Tyler: I never thought that the Holy Spirit and house renovation were so much alike. I have some work to do. See you next week. Bye.

Verse of the Day: Acts 1:8 (NIV) *But you shall receive power when the Holy Spirit has come upon you; and you shall be witnesses to Me in Jerusalem, and in all Judea and Samaria, and to the end of the earth.*

Memory Verse Talk: (use Holy Spirit Power Lesson 2, slide A)

One purpose of the baptism of the Holy Spirit is to give us power or boldness when we witness to others about our faith in Jesus Christ. Sometimes telling others about Jesus can make us timid or afraid, but the Holy Spirit can help us by giving us the words to say and the opportunities to say them. This verse also tells us where we should be witnesses for Christ. Most of us have never been to these places, but Jesus was speaking to the disciples who lived in Jerusalem. So we can insert places we know. For instance, Jerusalem would be places we are at all the time like our homes, our schools, and our neighborhoods. Judea would be like our city. So, we might find opportunities to witness to people in our city who don't go to our schools or live in our neighborhoods. Samaria would be the outsiders. Maybe there's a student at school that everyone picks on or someone with a disability, and nobody sits with him at lunch. These are also people we should find opportunities to tell about Jesus' love. The uttermost parts of the Earth means everywhere else. Some of you might grow up and take missions trips to other countries or become full-time missionaries. Even if you don't, you can pray for missionaries and give offerings for missions.

Memory Verse Activity: Chicken Egg Roll (use Holy Spirit Power Lesson 2, slide A)

Supplies needed: plastic eggs, strips of paper

Preparation: Place a slip of paper in each egg with words or phrases from the memory verse. Split the verses up depending on the number of students participating. If you have a larger group, you can split the students into different teams.

Each student will be given an egg. When the race begins, the student will roll the egg to the finish line with his or her nose (beak) only. When all the students finish, they will place the pieces of paper in order to show the memory verse.

Bible Story: The Holy Spirit Takes the Chicken Out of Peter

(Luke 22:31-34, 54-62; Acts 2:1-41)

Supplies needed: rubber chicken

When Jesus lived on the Earth, Peter was one of His most loyal disciples. Peter would do anything for Jesus. Shortly before Jesus was arrested, He told Peter that Peter would deny Him three times before the rooster crowed twice.

Peter was shocked. He told Jesus that even if everyone else deserted Him, Peter would go with Him even if it cost his life. Peter meant what he said. He loved Jesus and wanted to support Him, even if it cost Peter his life, but something happened.

Jesus was arrested and taken to trial. Peter followed and stood in the courtyard trying to figure out a way to help Jesus, but Peter was scared. Have you ever been so scared that you couldn't do something you really wanted to do? I believe we all have been that scared. Peter was afraid he was going to be arrested and killed. He stood around the fire hoping nobody recognized him.

That's when a young servant girl saw him. "This one has been with Jesus."

Peter was so terrified, he lied and said he didn't even know Jesus.

Another person came up to Peter and accused him of being one of Jesus' followers. Peter denied it again.

An hour passed, and Peter probably was starting to relax again when another person came up to him and accused him of being with Jesus. At this point, Peter was so afraid he swore and said he'd never heard of Jesus.

At that point, three things happened. First the rooster crowed twice. Then, as Jesus was marched through the courtyard by the soldiers, He looked at Peter. Peter was so distraught, he ran away and cried bitterly. When it had really mattered, he was a chicken and didn't stand with Jesus. Squeeze the rubber chicken.

After Jesus rose from the grave, He forgave Peter. A few weeks later, Peter was in the upper room where he and the other disciples were baptized in the Holy Spirit. When that happened, the Holy Spirit took the chicken out of Peter. Squeeze the rubber chicken.

He stood and witnessed to the whole crowd. Not only did he do that, but he told them that they were guilty of crucifying the Son of God. The people asked him what they could do, and Peter told them in Acts 2:28 (NKJV), "Repent, and let every one of you be baptized in the name of Jesus Christ for the remission of sins; and you shall receive the gift of the Holy Spirit."

Peter lived the rest of his life fearlessly telling other people about Jesus. When you're baptized in the Holy Spirit, the Holy Spirit will take the chicken out of you like he did for Peter and help you become a bold witness for Him.

Praise and Worship: Choose a couple of fast song and a slow song to lead children into praise and worship. It works well to talk to the children about what worship is and why it's important before you enter into this time. You can have a children's praise team, but until they understand leading praise and worship, have an adult leader or yourself be the worship leader.

Object Lesson:

1. The Holy Spirit is Stronger Than Our Fears

Supplies needed: rubber boat or toy that float, clear small bowl filled halfway with water, pitcher of water, tray to catch excess water

Have you ever been afraid of anything? What were you afraid of? Allow students to answer. *Those are some scary things.* Tell the students about things you were afraid of when you were younger.

Fear can be a good thing. We don't jump over a cliff because we're afraid of falling. We don't pick up poisonous snakes because we're afraid of getting bit. We don't touch hot stoves or fire because we're afraid of getting burned. Those are healthy fears that keep us safe. Fear is only bad when it's an unhealthy fear, when we're afraid of something that isn't really harmful, or when we don't do what God wants us to do because we're afraid. Those are the kind of fears the Holy Spirit can help us with.

Can you think of fears like that? Allow students to answer. If they can't think of any, make some suggestions.

Show the students the toy boat. *I'm going to call this boat the fear boat. Pretend this boat is full of all of your unhealthy fears.* Place the boat in the bowl of water. Start pouring the pitcher of water into the bowl. As you do this, continue talking. *The more we are filled with the Holy Spirit, the more the Holy Spirit will wash those fears away.* Keep pouring the water until the boat floats outside of the bowl.

2. The Power to Be Bold

Supplies needed: flashlight, batteries

Preparation: Make sure the batteries are not in the flashlight.

Have you ever been afraid of the dark? When I was young and my mom turned out the lights, I used to worry that a monster would come out of the shadows and get me. My mom gave me a flashlight so I could turn it on when I was afraid. Whenever I turned on the flashlight, I saw there weren't really monsters in my room.

Without Jesus in their lives, the people around me live in a dark world. There are times I really want to be a bold witness for Christ. I want my light to shine in the darkness, so I have here my trusty flashlight. Show flashlight. *I can shine this flashlight in the darkest of places, and it will light things up. When things are dark, I'm more likely to be afraid, but when things are lit up, my fears go away.*

That's because the light of the Holy Spirit overcomes the darkness.

Turn on flashlight. *I don't understand. Nothing happened. This flashlight should have the power to shine boldly in the darkness, but it doesn't. Do any of you have an idea what might be wrong?* Allow students to answer until one of the students says to check the batteries. Open up the flashlight and show there aren't any batteries in it.

No wonder my flashlight won't work. I don't have batteries in it. It's the batteries that give a flashlight the power to shine. Place the batteries in the flashlight and turn it on.

Just as the flashlight needs batteries to power it, I need the Holy Spirit to give me the power to be a light for Jesus in this dark world. Without the power of the Holy Spirit, I can't be a bold witness. I can't let my light shine.

Optional Object Lesson: Stay Connected to the Holy Spirit

Supplies needed: Steve Spangler Science Energy Stick

Have the students make an open circle. Place the energy stick in one hand and hold onto the hand of one of the students. Make sure the circle is open, and two people in the circle aren't holding hands. Have the students not holding hands close the circle by holding hands. The energy stick should light up.

When we are baptized in the Holy Spirit and are connected to Him, He gives us the power to become bold witnesses. But it's important to keep that connection and continually allow the Holy Spirit to fill you. If you break the connection, the Holy Spirit will no longer give you the boldness you need. Have two of the students in the circle break the circle by letting go of each other's hands.

We need to stay connected to the Holy Spirit. Have them hold hands again and complete the circle.

Message: The Holy Spirit Will Take the Chicken Out of You

(use Holy Spirit Power Lesson 2, slide B)

Supplies needed: rubber chicken

It's great to say that the Holy Spirit will take the chicken out of you, but it's harder when you want to talk to someone about Jesus and are afraid. What do you do when you're afraid that person might make fun of you? What about if it's in school and the teacher tells you that you can't talk about Jesus? What if your friend won't be your friend if you keep talking about Jesus? These are real things that can make you scared of telling others about Jesus. Those things have a spirit of fear on them. Squeeze rubber chicken.

Even though the spirit of fear can be strong, the Holy Spirit overcomes our fear and gives us boldness.

Show slide B and read the following verse. *2 Timothy 1:7 (NKJV) For God has not given us a spirit of fear, but of power and of love and of a sound mind.*

The Holy Spirit can give us the power to speak even when we are afraid. He conquers the spirit of fear because He is more powerful. He'll get rid of our fear. Another way to say it is the Holy Spirit will take the chicken in us. Throw the chicken over your shoulder.

The Holy Spirit is always with you. He is more powerful than any fear. Let me give you an example.

For this example, choose a young student and an older student. Ask a large adult from your church to help you with this example.

Have the young student stand out front. *Let's pretend this student wants to witness to her friends, but she's afraid. There's a bully in school who doesn't like Christians and gets other kids to make fun of them.*

Have the older student act threatening. *The younger student is afraid, she knows that the Holy Spirit lives inside of her. First, she prays.* Instruct the student to tell God she's afraid and that she needs the Holy Spirit to help you.

If she's baptized in the Holy Spirit, she'll begin to speak in tongues and worship to strengthen her inner spirit. She'll also remind herself that the Holy Spirit is more powerful than her fear. She'll say Bible verses like 1 John 4:4, "Greater is He that is within me than He that is in the world." Have the younger student repeat that phrase three or four times with convictions.

At this point, the large adult will stand in front of the smaller student and block the other student from getting to her. Encourage the other student not to give up, but the adult will always block him.

The Holy Spirit is greater than any fear or any bully that could come against us. Let's repeat 1 John 4:4 and shout like we really mean it. Have the students repeat "Greater is He that is within me than He that is within the world five or six times. Encourage them to shout the words.

Response Time

For response time, encourage students to be filled or refilled with the Holy Spirit. Play worship music, and lay hands on the students as you see God moving upon them. After worship, recap what God did for them.

Small Group Chat: Fear Not Picture Frames

Supplies needed: copies of Fear Not verses from Holy Spirit Power downloadable resources, cardstock, craft foam or optional craft picture frames, glue, markers, sticker, various craft decorations

Preparations: Make a copy of Fear Not verses for each student. Use 8 ½ by 11 inch size cardstock to glue Fear Not verses papers. Make sure they are centered on the cardstock.

Have students cut out and glue craft foam around the edges of the card stock to create a picture frame. Let them decorate their frames.

While the students are decorating their picture frames, go over the Fear Not verses. Let the students know they can hang these verses in their bedrooms or in their lockers at school to remind them the Holy Spirit is with them, and they don't have to be afraid.

Lesson 3 - The Holy Spirit Helps Us

Focus Point: The Holy Spirit helps us.

Goal: Students will learn that the Holy Spirit was sent by God to come alongside us and help us in a variety of ways.

Verse of the Day: John 14:16 (NKJV) *And I will pray the Father, and He will give you another Helper, that He may abide with you forever.*

Supplies Needed:

- doctor puppet or doctor costume for skit
- portable toolbox with various tools
- Tyler the Power Tool Guy Skit: Tyler wears a portable toolbox or toolbelt with various tools and is dressed in blue jeans and a plaid shirt, etc.
- blueprints
- chairs
- Signs with the following written on them with a colorful marker: Holy Spirit Boldness, Holy Spirit Knowledge, Holy Spirit Wisdom, Holy Spirit Deliverance
- drinking straw
- string
- tape
- balloon
- ink pad
- paper
- wipe
- tennis racket or other sports equipment

Opening: *Power Tools Countdown* (optional) or *Power Tools* Slide

Welcome:

Welcome. This month, we've been learning about the Holy Spirit. Today, we're going to learn about one of the main jobs of the Holy Spirit. The Holy Spirit lives in us to help us. There are many ways the Holy Spirit helps us, and we're going to learn some of those ways in this lesson.

Prayer: Ask a child to pray over the service.

Rules: (use rules slide) Go over the 5 Ups Rules.

Go over the *5 Ups Rules*: 1. Sit up straight. 2. Listen up. 3. Hush up. 4. Don't get up and run around or go to the bathroom. 5. Worship Up! (stand up and participate during praise and worship)

Theme or Activity Songs: Choose one of two fast moving activity or theme songs that go with the curriculum.

Game Time: Fruit Basket (use game time slide)

Supplies needed: chairs

Preparation: Arrange chairs in a circle facing the center. Have one chair for each student.

Stand in the center of the circle and have the students sit in the chairs. Assign each player to be a fruit. Have three or more fruits to assign. It is preferable to have at least three to five students be assigned to each fruit. Increase the number of fruits to accomplish that. Encourage the students to remember which fruit they are.

The object of the game is to have the center person call out the name of a fruit. All students who were assigned that fruit must stand and find another seat. You call out the fruit first and sit so one of the students doesn't have a chair to sit in. That student is the next to call out a fruit.

When the students get the hang of the game, stand and allow all the students to sit. Explain that when Fruit Basket is called out, all of the students must find another seat. Let them know they can't sit in the seat next to them. Call out Fruit Basket, and sit in one of the seats. Continue the game.

One way the Holy Spirit helps us is to enable us to make us fruity Christian. The Holy Spirt fruit that He wants us to have is love, joy, peace, longsuffering, goodness, kindness, faithfulness, gentleness, and self-control. The more we allow the Holy Spirit to fill us and help us, the more this fruit will show in our lives.

Memory Verse Skit: (use Holy Spirit Power Lesson 3, slide A)

Supplies needed: doctor puppet or doctor costume for skit

Doctor Word: Hi kids. I'm Doctor Word. I'm called that because I'm a doctor and because I love the Word of God. Being a doctor is a difficult job. I have to remember a lot of things I learned in medical school. I have to remember the symptoms for every disease and how to treat the disease once I diagnose it. I'm so grateful I have the Holy Spirit to help and guide me along the way. When I'm treating a patient, I sometimes feel the Holy Spirit has come alongside me to help me know what to do. That's why today's memory verse is so important to me. John 14:16 (NKJV) says, *"And I will pray the Father, and He will give you another Helper, that He may abide with you forever."* Imagine that. Jesus prayed for us to have the Holy Spirit to stay with us forever and to help us. That's comforting.

Offering: The Holy Spirit Helps Us Know What to Give

Did you know the Holy Spirit can help you know how much to give? Tell a story about how the Holy Spirit urged you to give a certain amount in the offering, and how it impacted you. Or tell how you needed something (food, money), and the Holy Spirit urged someone else to give you just what you needed.

Skit: Tyler the Power Tool Guy Has a Plan

Supplies Needed: blueprints or plans. Tyler has a portable toolbox or toolbelt with various tools and is dressed in blue jeans and a plaid shirt, etc. If you use a girl in the skit, have her dress the same and call her Tyler the Power Tool Gal.

Tyler the Power Tool Guy: (Comes in and starts pouring over plans) Okay, if I extended it here, I'd have to decrease it there.

Leader: Hi, Tyler. What's going on? Do you have any special power tools to show us today?

Tyler: Not today. Today, I have something much more powerful than a power tool.

Leader: More powerful than a power tool? I can't believe you said that. What is this thing more powerful than a power tool?

Tyler: I have the blueprints to the house I'm renovating and the plans for what I'm going my renovation.

Leader: How are those papers more important than a power tool?

Tyler: These plans and blueprints guide and help me. If I build an island and don't look at the plans first, the island might be too big to fit in the kitchen. Or I might buy a bathtub that's two inches too long for the bathtub area.

Leader: I never thought of that.

Tyler: These plans help me in other ways too. Suppose I want to tear down a wall. If the wall is load bearing, meaning it supports the whole upstairs, I can't tear it down without installing a beam to support it. Having these plans to help and guide me is the most important part of renovating a house.

Leader: So, those plans are sort of like the Holy Spirit.

Tyler: How can house plans be like the Holy Spirit.

Leader: The Holy Spirit guides us and helps us in every area of our life. He even helps us understand the Bible.

Tyler: In that case, you're right. The Holy Spirit is like these house plans. I have to go. I'm meeting with the project manager to go over these plans.

(Exits)

Verse of the Day: John 14:16 (NKJV) *And I will pray the Father, and He will give you another Helper, that He may abide with you forever.*

Memory Verse Talk: (use Holy Spirit Power Lesson 3, slide A)

Imagine having someone come alongside you all the time and help you whenever you need it. When you need to remember something, that helper will help you remember. When you need strength or the ability to do something, that helper will give you that ability. When you are upset, that helper will comfort you. When you need wisdom or guidance, that helper will guide you. When you need to know the right thing to do, the helper will let you know.

It doesn't take much to imagine this because if you're a Christian, you already have a helper like this.

The Holy Spirit is your helper who is always with you.

Memory Verse Activity: Help Each Other

Have your students pair up. Each pair should have an older student and a younger student. The older student teaches the younger student the verse. When you're done, have the younger students say the verse.

I split you into pairs so one of you could help the other learn the memory verse. Was this helpful? Allow students to answer. *The Holy Spirit also wants to help you remember Scripture because The Holy Spirit is always with us to help us.*

Bible Story: The Holy Spirit Helps Peter and John

(Acts 4:1-31)

Supplies needed: Signs with the following written on them with a colorful marker: Holy Spirit Boldness, Holy Spirit Knowledge, Holy Spirit Wisdom, Holy Spirit Deliverance. Write in pencil on the back what each sign says so you can easily find the right sign.

The disciples, Peter and John, went to the temple and found a crippled man there. They healed him in the name of Jesus, and he started walking, leaping and praising God. This made everyone interested in hearing what Peter and John had to say, so they preached the Gospel.

Soon, they were arrested and brought before the temple leaders. They weren't arrested for stealing or hurting others. They were arrested because they were doing something good. They were telling others about Jesus and how He died for our sins and rose again. Some people listened to Peter and John and invited Jesus to be their Savior and Lord. This made the temple leaders angry. That's why they arrested Peter and John. They put them in prison overnight.

Ask the students if they've ever been told they can't talk about Jesus. The students who go to public school have probably been told this at some point.

The next day, the leaders brought in Peter and John and questioned them. They asked, "By what power or what name did you do this?"

Show Holy Spirit Boldness sign.

Scripture says that Peter was filled with the Holy Spirit and stood up to the leaders even though they might send him to prison. He told them all about Jesus and how they had healed a lame man in the name of Jesus.

Show Holy Spirit Knowledge sign.

The leaders were amazed. They knew Peter and John weren't educated men, but they knew the Scriptures and what they meant. This was because the Holy Spirit helped them by teaching them about God's Word.

Show Holy Spirit Wisdom sign.

The leaders threatened Peter and John and told them not to teach or preach in the name of Jesus again.

The Holy Spirit helped Peter and John by giving them wisdom about what to say. In Acts 4:19-20 (NIV), But Peter and John replied, "Which is right in God's eyes: to listen to you, or to him? You be the judges! As for us, we cannot help speaking about what we have seen and heard."

Show Holy Spirit Deliverence sign.

The Holy Spirit helped Peter and John by delivered them from prison. The temple leaders couldn't figure out how to punish them since a man had been miraculously healed, so they let them go.

In difficult times, the Holy Spirit will help you just as He helped Peter and John.

Praise and Worship: Choose a couple of fast song and a slow song to lead children into praise and worship. It works well to talk to the children about what worship is and why it's important before you enter into this time. You can have a children's praise team, but until they understand leading praise and worship, have an adult leader or yourself be the worship leader.

Object Lessons:

1. **The Holy Spirit Guides Us** (use Holy Spirit Lesson 3, slides B, C, D, and E)

Supplies needed: drinking straw, string, tape, balloon, ink pad, paper, wipe

Preparation: Thread the string through the straw before the demonstration.

Show Slide B. *One way the Holy Spirit helps us is by guiding us into all truth. John 16:13 (NIV) says, "But when he, the Spirit of truth, comes, he will guide you into all the truth."*

Give an illustration about how that happens. Choose two students to help you. One student will hold one end of the string. Blow up the balloon or have the other student blow it up. Tell the student to aim it at the other student and let go. The balloon will not reach its target. Have the student try a couple more times. Explain that, without the Holy Spirit guiding us, we can't get where we need to be.

Blow the balloon up again. This time, tape it to the straw. Explain that the straw acts in the same way as the Holy Spirit. Hold on to the other end of the string, and have the student let go of the balloon. The balloon will reach the other student. *The Holy Spirit will guide you if you let Him.*

Sometimes, Christians have a hard time understanding how the Holy Spirit can guide us when He doesn't speak out loud and we can't see Him. We tell you to listen to the Holy Spirit and do what He tells you, but sometimes, we forget to tell you how to listen to the Holy Spirit. The Holy Spirit rarely speaks in a voice you can hear out loud, but He lives inside your spirit, and He does speak to our spirit and impress things upon us.

Show the students the stamp pad. Place your finger on the pad and press it onto the paper. Show the students your fingerprint. Use the wipe to wipe the ink off your finger. *I have an impression of my finger on this paper. It doesn't look exactly like my finger, but it does show the imprint of my finger. It's my fingerprint. An impression is sort of like that. The Holy Spirit impresses something on the inside of you. You don't have a clear picture of what He wants, but you do have an impression. From that impression, you can figure out how the Holy Spirit wants to guide you. You have a Holy Spirit print on your spirit.*

Show slide C. *One way the Holy Spirit guides us or impresses us is to help us understand God's Word. John 14:26 (NIV) say, "But the Advocate, the Holy Spirit, whom the Father will send in my name, will teach you all things and will remind you of everything I have said to you." Sometimes, He'll remind us what the Word of God says. Other times, He'll show us what the verses mean.*

Another way the Holy Spirit guides us is to bears witness with our spirits so we know what is right and what is wrong. Some people say you should let your conscious be your guide. That works most of the time when we know what is right and what is wrong, but sometimes we need help.

Show Slide D. Ezekiel 36:27 (NIV) says, "I will put my Spirit inside you. And I will help you live by my rules. You will be careful to obey my laws."

The Holy Spirit does that in two ways. First, He'll show you what is right and what is wrong. Second, He'll show you when you've done something wrong so you can ask God to forgive you.

A third way the Holy Spirit guides us is to give us wisdom. Wisdom is different than knowledge. Knowledge is knowing facts. Wisdom shows us what to do in hard situations.

Show Slide E. *James 1:5 (NIV) says, "If any of you lacks wisdom, you should ask God, who gives generously to all without finding fault, and it will be given to you."*

So if you don't know what to do, you can ask the Holy Spirit, and He will guide you with His wisdom.

2. Object Lesson: The Holy Spirit Comforts Us

Supplies needed: comforter or blanket

Have your students raise their hands if any of the following things have happened to them.

Have you ever been sad? Have you ever had a pet or a grandparent or someone close to you die? Have you even been upset because you lost a friend either because the friend moved away or because he stopped being your friend? Have you ever heard your parents yell at each other, and it scared you? Have you ever had a bad dream? Have you ever had anyone bully you? Have you ever been sick? Have you ever been accused of doing something you didn't do? Have you ever been treated unfairly?

Here's the last question. Raise your hand if you would answer yes to any of these questions? Keep your hands raised and look around. All of us have had many of these things happen to us.

This is my comforter from when I was little. Tell a story about when you were little how getting under a blanket of comforter would make you feel better when you were upset, or sick, or sad, or even angry. *Some children use blankets or comforters to make a tent over a table or a desk. They feel safe and comforted hiding under their tent blankets. Some don't use comforters. They hug stuffed animals, or they go to a special place in their yard or home that makes them feel better. Some like to listen to music, read stories, and draw pictures.*

How many of you have something you use to comfort you? Allow student to answer. Ask the students who want to what they use to comfort them.

All those things you mentioned are wonderful comforters, but the Holy Spirit is even a better comforter. Tell about a time in your life when the Holy Spirit comforted you during a hard time. *The Holy Spirit makes you feel better when you're sad, and He heals those sad feelings. He can even help you know how to handle these bad situations. The Holy Spirit is the best comforter there is.*

Message: The Holy Spirit Helps Us

Supplies needed: tennis racket or other sports equipment

When I was younger, I decided I wanted to play tennis professionally. I took tennis lessons, and I watched videos on how to play tennis. My parents even hired a coach to help me know how to play better. I practiced for hours, but no matter how hard I tried, I was never good enough to play professionally. So, I gave up professional tennis. Now, I just play for fun.

Imagine if I hired the most famous tennis player ever to teach me, someone like Serena Williams or Rodger Federer. Do you think I could become as good as that tennis player? I don't. I might get a little better, but I'd never be as good as them. But imagine if that tennis player could somehow get inside of me and play the game through me. If that were to happen, I could become a professional tennis player because I wouldn't be playing the game with my abilities. I'd have their abilities.

That's what the Holy Spirit does. He lives inside of you, and the more you cooperate with Him, the more He can operate through you. You don't have to do it alone or try with your own abilities. You have the Holy Spirit to help you, guide you, comfort you, and live the Christian life through you.

Response Time:

Pray a general pray and ask the Holy Spirit to help and guide the students. Then lead the students into seeking the Holy Spirit. Encourage students to be filled or refilled with the Holy Spirit. Play worship music, and lay hands on the students as you see God moving upon them. After worship, recap what God did for them.

Small Group Chat: Holy Spirit Helpers

Read 2 Corinthians 1:3-4 (ICB). *Praise be to the God and Father of our Lord Jesus Christ. God is the Father who is full of mercy. And he is the God of all comfort. He comforts us every time we have trouble, so that we can comfort others when they have trouble. We can comfort them with the same comfort that God gives us.*

Explain to the students that just as the Holy Spirit helps us and comforts us, He wants us to help others and comfort them. In a way, the Holy Spirit wants us to be His helpers.

Have the students make suggestions about how they can help the Holy Spirit by helping others. Encourage them to find someone to help this week. Have them ask the Holy Spirit to show them who they can help. Encourage them to write down what happened and share it next week during church.

Lesson 4: The Holy Spirit Reveals Things

Focus Point: The Holy Spirit reveals things to us.

Goal: Students will learn the Holy Spirit reveals things to them in a variety of ways.

Verse of the Day: Acts 2:17 (NIV) *"In the last days," God says, "I will pour out my Spirit on all people. Your sons and daughters will prophesy, your young men will see visions, your old men will dream dreams."*

Supplies Needed:

- doctor puppet or doctor costume for skit
- portable toolbox with various tools
- Tyler the Power Tool Guy Skit: Tyler wears a portable toolbox or toolbelt with various tools and is dressed in blue jeans and a plaid shirt, etc.
- optional: electric stud finder
- beanbag or ball
- sound effects of a storm (optional)
- radio
- Bible
- rubber or toy ear
- cross
- battery tester
- batteries

Opening: *Power Tools Countdown* (optional) or *Power Tools* Slide

Welcome: Holy Spirit Reveals Things

Welcome. During small group last week, you were all encouraged to find someone to help just as the Holy Spirit helps us. Did any of you do this? Allow students to tell their stories. *When you saw who needed your help, it was the Holy Spirit revealing these people to you. That's what we're going to talk about today. The Holy Spirit reveals things to us.*

Prayer: Have a student pray over the service.

Rules: (use rules slide) Go over the 5 Ups Rules.

Go over the *5 Ups Rules*: 1. Sit up straight. 2. Listen up. 3. Hush up. 4. Don't get up and run around or go to the bathroom. 5. Worship Up! (stand up and participate during praise and worship)

Theme or Activity Songs: Choose one of two fast moving activity or theme songs that go with the curriculum.

Game Time: I Spy (use game time slide)

Supplies needed: none

Play the I Spy game with your students. Choose an object you can see. Try to choose something hard to guess. Say, "I spy with my little eye something (choose a color). Students will take turns asking questions or making guesses until someone guesses correctly. The student who guesses gets to pick the object next.

When the game is over, tell your students that just as you gave hints such as the color to reveal the object, the Holy Spirit wants to reveal things to us.

Memory Verse Skit: (use Holy Spirit Power Lesson 4, slide A)

Supplies needed: doctor puppet or doctor costume for skit

Doctor Word: Hi kids. I'm Doctor Word. I'm called that because I'm a doctor and because I love the Word of God. You would think doctors know everything about medicine, but sometimes we have cases that stump us. One time, I had a patient that presented symptoms for Covid. I tested him three or four times, but he always tested negative. At first, I thought he might have a common flu virus, but his symptoms got worse. I tested for pneumonia and bronchitis, and I tried antibiotics. Nothing worked. I prayed and asked God what I should do. That night, I had a dream. During the dream, I saw the patient. He turned to me and said, "I have Respiratory System Virus." Then I woke up. I knew God gave me that dream to reveal what was wrong with my patient. RSV can be a serious illness for babies and older patients, but it's often mistaken for something else and has the same symptoms as Covid. When I knew what was wrong, I knew how to treat my patient. God reveals things to us in a variety of ways. Our verse for today is Acts 2:17 (NIV). *"In the last days," God says, "I will pour out my Spirit on all people. Your sons and daughters will prophesy, your young men will see visions, your old men will dream dreams."*

Offering: How Much Should I Give?

We should always give a tithe in the offering. A tithe is ten percent of whatever we make. So, if you get a ten-dollar allowance, you should give one dollar. Sometimes God will reveal to us that He wants us to give more that the ten percent. He gives us an impression of how much money we should give in the offering. When He does that, if we obey Him, He will bless us.

Skit: Tyler the Power Tool Guy's Revealing Power Tool

Supplies Needed: optional: electric stud finder. Tyler has a portable toolbox or toolbelt with various tools and is dressed in blue jeans and a plaid shirt, etc. If you use a girl in the skit, have her dress the same and call her Tyler the Power Tool Gal.

Tyler the Power Tool Guy: (Comes in) I hear that your teaching today about the Holy Spirit revealing things you can't see.

Leader: That's right, Tyler.

Tyler: That's great. Today, I want to tell you about a power tool that reveals things you can't see.

Leader: That's amazing. What power tool is that?

Tyler: (optional: shows stud finder) It's an electric stud finder.

Leader: An electric stud finder? What does that do?

Tyler: Part of the renovation involves hanging pictures. To do that, I need to find the studs or wood behind the walls. I could do that by knocking on the walls until I find the wood, but with a stud finder, I don't have to do that. I can use the stud finder to find the wood beams holding up the wall that I can't see.

Leader: That's amazing. So this stud find reveals things you can't see just like the Holy Spirit reveals things we don't know.

Tyler: That's right. I think I'm going to rename it. I'm going to call it my power wood revealer. I have to go now.

(Exits)

Verse of the Day: Acts 2:17 (NIV) *"In the last days," God says, "I will pour out my Spirit on all people. Your sons and daughters will prophesy, your young men will see visions, your old men will dream dreams."*

Memory Verse Talk: (use Holy Spirit Power Lesson 4, slide A)

Supplies needed: none

Acts 2:17 (NIV) says, "In the last days," God says, "I will pour out my Spirit on all people. Your sons and daughters will prophesy, your young men will see visions, your old men will dream dreams."

Because of this Scripture, we know the Holy Spirit sometimes reveals things to us in prophesy, visions, and dreams. Prophesy is when the Holy Spirit speaks through someone. Visions are when the Holy Spirit shows us things through pictures or images. Sometimes visions will be so real, it will be like we're watching something happen. Dreams are when the Holy Spirit shows us something in a dream, not just anytime we remember our dreams. We'll talk more about these later, but the important thing to remember is there's no age limit on this. If you are a Christian, God may choose to reveal things to you through any of these methods.

Memory Verse Activity: Memory Verse Hot Potato

Supplies needed: beanbag or ball

Rehearse the verse a few times. Have the students play a game of hot potato. They will arrange their chairs in a circle. Start the game by saying the verse address and passing the beanbag to one of the students. That student will say the first word in the verse when the beanbag and pass the beanbag to the next student who will say the second word of the verse. Continue passing the beanbag around the circle until the verse has been said several times. If it takes a student more than three seconds to say the next word, that student is out.

Bible Story: Prophecy, Dreams, and Visions

(Acts 27; Acts 16:1-10; Acts 22:6-10)

Supplies needed: sound effects of a storm (optional)

Sometimes even adults have a hard time understanding prophecy, dreams, and visions, so we're going to look at three stories in the book of Acts where God revealed things to the Apostle Paul using prophecy, dreams, visions, and other methods.

Turn on storm sound effects. *In Acts 27, Paul was aboard a ship as a prisoner headed to Rome. The weather started getting bad, and the sailing became dangerous. Paul felt an impression from the Holy Spirit and told the leaders on the ship to dock in Crete or the storm would become even more dangerous. God revealed this to Paul through a Word of Knowledge. A Word of Knowledge is when God reveals something to you that you wouldn't know otherwise.*

The leaders didn't listen, and the storm got worse. Things got so bad that everyone thought they were going to die. At this point, God gave Paul a vision and a prophetic word. This is what Paul heard and said in verses 23-26 (NIV). "Last night an angel of the God to whom I belong and whom I serve stood beside me and said, 'Do not be afraid, Paul. You must stand trial before Caesar; and God has graciously given you the lives of all who sail with you.' So keep up your courage, men, for I have faith in God that it will happen just as he told me. Nevertheless, we must run aground on some island."

This encouraged and comforted the men on the ship. Fourteen days later, they were saved when the ship ran aground on the island of Malta. God had saved everyone on the ship.

Another time, *in Acts 16, Paul and his companions were traveling the countryside telling people about Jesus. Every time they tried to go in a certain direction, the Holy Spirit impressed upon them not to go that way. Sometimes, the Holy Spirit will give us discernment, an uneasy feeling in our sprits, to show us we shouldn't go somewhere or do something. That's what happened to Paul. Finally, they stopped for the night and went to sleep. While they were sleeping, Paul had a dream. In his dream, he saw a man from Macedonia saying, "Come over here and help us." Paul knew the Holy Spirit gave him that dream because they were supposed to head in that direction. Sometimes God shows us things in our dreams. You'll know when you have a God dream because you'll remember the dream in detail, and you'll feel a stirring in your spirit. If you don't know what your God dream means, ask the Holy Spirit to reveal the meaning. If you still are unsure, ask an adult you trust to help you.*

Paul had many visions in his lifetime. I'm going to tell you what happened when he was given the first vision he ever had. It happened when Paul was younger. He hated Christians and was trying to kill them or arrest them. He was on the road to Damascus when he saw a vision.

In Acts 22:6-10 NIV, Paul told leaders in Jerusalem his vision. This is what he said. "About noon as I came near Damascus, suddenly a bright light from heaven flashed around me. I fell to the ground and heard a voice say to me, 'Saul! Saul! Why do you persecute me?'

"'Who are you, Lord?' I asked.

"'I am Jesus of Nazareth, whom you are persecuting,' he replied.

"My companions saw the light, but they did not understand the voice of him who was speaking to me.

"'What shall I do, Lord?' I asked.

"'Get up,' the Lord said, 'and go into Damascus. There you will be told all that you have been assigned to do."

When Paul saw that vision, he gave his life to God.

Just as the Holy Spirit revealed things to Paul in prophecy, dreams, vision, words of knowledge, discernment, and impressions, the Holy Spirit will reveal things to you if you listen to Him, not with your ears but with your spirit.

Praise and Worship: Choose a couple of fast song and a slow song to lead children into praise and worship. It works well to talk to the children about what worship is and why it's important before you enter into this time. You can have a children's praise team, but until they understand leading praise and worship, have an adult leader or yourself be the worship leader.

Object Lessons:

1. Hearing God's Voice

Supplies needed: radio, Bible, rubber or toy ear (optional: show your own ear), cross

Show radio. *Do any of you have a radio? Most people have a radio in their car or on their alarm clocks, but people don't listen to the radio as much as they used to. When I was young (or my mom or grandma was young depending on your age), cell phones were something most kids didn't have, and even if they did, they couldn't listen to music on them. Most kids listened to CD players (cassette players, record players, eight-track players) or the radio when the wanted to listen to music.*

Turn on the radio. *Sometimes, if reception was bad, all you could get was static. You had to try to tune the radio in order to get the right station.* Tune the radio so it gets static, then tune it to a station.

Listening to the Holy Spirit when He reveals things is a lot like tuning a radio. Sometimes it's hard to understand what He is saying, but as we tune our spiritual ears and listen to His voice, we will get a clearer signal on what he is trying to say.

John 16:13-14 (NIV) gives a few guidelines for tuning into the Holy Spirit. "But when he, the Spirit of truth, comes, he will guide you into all the truth. He will not speak on his own; he will speak only what he hears, and he will tell you what is yet to come. He will glorify me because it is from me that he will receive what he will make known to you."

Show Bible. *The Holy Spirit guides us in truth. He will never tell us anything that goes against the Word of God.*

Show rubber or toy ear or point to your own ear. *The Holy Spirit only tells us what He hears from God the Father and God the Son. If you're hearing something that would cause you to sin or doubt God, you are tuning into the wrong channel.*

Show cross. *The Holy Spirit glorifies Jesus. Anything the Holy Spirit tells you will lift up and glorify Jesus in your life.*

Another way to know if you are hearing right is to pray. Ask God to give you wisdom and discernment about what you're hearing. When you do this, if what you are hearing is of the Holy Spirit, you'll get a stronger signal. Tune radio to a strong signal. *If not, the signal will fade.* Tune radio to static.

Another way is to talk to a spiritual leader in your life. Suggest certain people you have talked to ahead of time. Choose leaders who understand God speaks to children.

2. Object Lesson: Prophetic Tester

Supplies needed: battery tester, batteries

Show battery tester. *This is a battery tester. When I want to know if a battery has a charge, I use it to test the battery.* Demonstrate the battery tester on the batteries and tell your students how much of a charge each battery has.

Did you know the Holy Spirit gives you a prophecy tester and wants you to use it? That tester is called discernment.

1 Thessalonians 5:20-21 says, "Do not treat prophecies with contempt but test them all; hold on to what is good,"

Here's how to use your discernment. Whenever there is a prophecy, vision, dream, or word of knowledge, whether it is given to you or if you are the one who receives the prophecy, ask God to help you use your discernment detector. Here's some questions you should ask:

Does it lift up Jesus?

Does it confirm what the Bible says?

Does it set well with what the Holy Spirit is telling you? Sometimes someone will try to give you a word that goes against what the Holy Spirit is telling you even though it doesn't go against Scripture. I'll give you an example. The Holy Spirit has led me to be a children's pastor. If someone prophecies that I should stop being a children's pastor and become a missionary in China, I will ask God if I'm wrong about what He is saying to me or if the prophecy is wrong? If God is telling me to be a children's pastor, the Holy Spirit won't tell someone to tell me to do something else instead. The Holy Spirit will speak to me first as long as I'm listening to Him and confirm what He's saying with a prophetic word.

There is one more discernment test. This is found in 1 Corinthians 14:3 (NKJ). "But he who prophesies speaks edification and exhortation and comfort to men."

Edification means to lift someone to become stronger spiritually. Things like you don't have what it takes to be a strong Christian would always be a false prophecy.

Exhortation means encouraging someone to grow closer to God. That means somebody isn't going to prophecy that I should worship or read my Bible so much.

Comfort means to comfort or encourage someone. If a prophecy tears you down or discourages you, it is a false prophecy.

What happens if someone gives a prophecy that you detect isn't from the Holy Spirit. Always operate in love. Love is more important in the Kingdom of God than prophecy. First, pray for the person. Second, talk to an adult you trust. Recommend leaders you've talked to ahead of time. *Third, declare that you don't receive that prophecy, but most of the time, you don't want to say it out loud in front of the person. You may want to get alone to say this or say it in a quiet voice only God can hear.*

As you operate in the prophetic more, it will be easier to know what is the Holy Spirit and what isn't. Trust the Holy Spirit to lead you, and talk to adults you trust.

Message: Listening to the Holy Spirit

Preparation: This message asks you to talk about times the Holy Spirit has revealed things in your life. If you have areas where you don't have experience, ask adults in your congregation to give testimonies and examples for these things. If you can, choose leaders that you approve to guide students in the prophetic.

The Holy Spirit wants to reveal things to you. He does this in a variety of ways.

The most important way the Holy Spirit reveals things to us is through the Word of God. The more we learn the Word of God, the more the Holy Spirit will show us what it means and how to apply it to our lives. Tell about a time God has done this in your life.

Another way the Holy Spirit reveals things is to impress things on us in our spirits. Tell about a time God has done this in your life.

The Holy Spirit gives us Words of Wisdom and Words of Knowledge. This is when we know something or we know what to do about something even though there's no way we could know if the Holy Spirit didn't show us. Tell about a time God has done this in your life.

The Holy Spirit gives us dreams. We sometimes have dreams that are just dreams, but sometimes the Holy Spirit will show us things in our dreams. Tell about a time God has done this in your life.

The Holy Spirit gives us visions. Visions sometimes are pictures that come to our mind that we know the Holy Spirit shows us. Sometimes visions are just an impression of an image, and sometimes visions are so strong we can feel like we are really seeing something or experiencing something. This is called an open vision. Tell about a time God has done this in your life.

The Holy Spirit gives us prophetic messages to speak to people. Sometimes, these messages are an image or just a few words. Other times, the Holy Spirit gives us entire sentences to speak or a Scripture. Tell about a time God has done this in your life.

The Holy Spirit revelations are not always easy to interpret or tune in, but as we learn to listen to the Holy Spirit, it's easier to operate in the prophetic. Ask an adult you trust to help you connect what you're hearing to Scripture and to know if you are hearing right, and don't be afraid of making a mistake. That's the only way to learn.

Response Time:

Preparation: Ask the adult leaders you've chosen from your congregation who are spiritual to help you with this.

Explain to your students that we are going to pray for the Holy Spirit. to use us prophetically. Have students who have been baptized in the Holy Spirit pray in tongues. Have the other students pray and worship in their native language.

After praying for a while, ask your adult volunteers to sit in chairs in front. Ask your students if any of them have a word or an image to speak to any of the adults. Encourage them if they're timid at first. You may have to give an example by having an adult give a word. As the students do this, allow the Holy Spirit to lead you as you interpret these words according to Scripture. If an adult volunteer wants to add information to any of the words spoken, encourage them to do so. This will encourage students to speak when they have a word in a safe way and place without worrying about harsh judgement.

At the end, encourage students to go to you, their parents, or one of these volunteers when they have a message from the Holy Spirit. In this way, they will grow in the prophetic while learning to hear the Holy Spirit more effectively.

Small Group Chat: Picture This

Supplies needed: paper, colored pencils or markers

Have the students draw pictures of things the Holy Spirit is showing them. Allow them to show these pictures and talk about them.

Encourage the students to have a notebook with them at all times, even at night, so they can write or draw what the Holy Spirit is showing them.

Lesson 5: The Holy Spirit Gives Us His Power

Focus Point: The Holy Spirit works through us with His power.

Goal: Students will learn they can heal and perform miracles when they do so with the power of the Holy Spirit.

Verse of the Day: Zechariah 4:6b (NIV) *"Not by might nor by power, but by my Spirit," says the Lord Almighty.*

Supplies Needed:

- doctor puppet or doctor costume for skit
- portable toolbox with various tools
- Tyler the Power Tool Guy Skit: Tyler wears a portable toolbox or toolbelt with various tools and is dressed in blue jeans and a plaid shirt, etc.
- small power tool
- a balloon for each student
- duct tape or string
- basketball
- ping pong ball
- hair dryer
- 2 name tags
- marker
- olive oil or essential oil

Opening: *Power Tools Countdown* (optional) or *Power Tools* Slide

Welcome: Holy Spirit Power

Welcome. For the last four weeks, we've been learning about Holy Spirit Power. We've learned we can receive power through the baptism of the Holy Spirit. We've learned the Holy Spirit gives us boldness, helps us, and reveals things to us. Today, we are going to learn more about the power of the Holy Spirit and how He can do miraculous things through us.

Prayer: Have a student pray over the service.

Rules: (use rules slide) Go over the 5 Ups Rules.

Go over the *5 Ups Rules*: 1. Sit up straight. 2. Listen up. 3. Hush up. 4. Don't get up and run around or go to the bathroom. 5. Worship Up! (stand up and participate during praise and worship)

Theme or Activity Songs: Choose one of two fast moving activity or theme songs that go with the curriculum.

Game Time: A Mighty Rushing Balloon (use game time slide)

Supplies needed: a balloon for each student, duct tape or string

Preparation: Make a large circle with duct tape or string.

You might want to ask your students questions about the previous Holy Spirit Power lessons to decide who participates, or if you have a smaller group, everyone could participate.

Explain to the students how the game is played. Each student playing will receive a deflated balloon. They will stand back to back in the center of the duct tape circle. When the leader says go, each one will blow up his balloon and let go of it allowing it to deflate. The student will then stand where his balloon landed. The first student to escape the circle wins.

It was almost impossible to get the balloon to go where you want it no matter how hard you try. We can't control the Holy Spirit by using our power or might. We can only cooperate with the Holy Spirit. When He moves, we move with Him.

Memory Verse Skit: (use Holy Spirit Power Lesson 4, slide A)

Supplies needed: doctor puppet or doctor costume for skit

Doctor Word: Hi kids. I'm Doctor Word. I'm called that because I'm a doctor and because I love the Word of God. One of the hardest things to get used to as a doctor is that I can't cure everyone. No matter how hard I try or how much I learn, I don't have the power to heal people. Only the Holy Spirit has that power. That's why today's memory verse is so important to me. Zechariah 4:6b (NIV) says, *"'Not by might nor by power, but by my Spirit,' says the Lord Almighty."* The Holy Spirit is the one who has the power to miraculously heal and do miracles.

Offering: Multiplication

Did you know that when you give in the offering, God has the power to multiply your offering? That's right. I know this because in John 6, the disciples told Jesus that they didn't have enough food to feed the multitudes that had come to hear Jesus speak. A boy offered his lunch, but it was only five small loaves of bread and two small fish. Jesus blessed it and had the disciples pass out the food. Jesus multiplied the boy's offering. It not only fed all 5,000 people, but there were twelve large baskets of food left over.

Skit: Tyler the Power Tool Guy Greatest Job

Supplies Needed: small power tool, Tyler has a portable toolbox or toolbelt with various tools and is dressed in blue jeans and a plaid shirt, etc. If you use a girl in the skit, have her dress the same and call her Tyler the Power Tool Gal.

Tyler the Power Tool Guy: (Comes in carrying a small power tool) This is my favorite job ever.

Leader: Hi, Tyler. Are you still renovating that old house?

Tyler: I sure am. It's been a lot of fun.

Leader: What makes this job better than you're other jobs?

Tyler: (shows power tool) Are you kidding me? I get to use so many of my power tools.

Leader: That's awesome. I know you love your power tools. Which power tools have you used so far?

Tyler: I do love my power tools. I got to use a chainsaw and jackhammer for cutting out walls, floors, and cabinets. I got to use my jigsaw for cutting out door and window frames and my circular saw for cutting wood planks for beams and fireplace mantles. I used my drill for screws and my nail gun for nails. I used other power tools too, but there isn't enough time to mention them all. Ahh. God is good to me.

Leader: I'm so happy for you. When will the job be finished?

Tyler: I started five weeks ago. I should be done in another week or two.

Leader: That's fast for everything you had to do.

Tyler: Not really. That's fairly typical.

Leader: I'm curious. In the past, people didn't have power tools. How did they renovate or build houses then.

Tyler: You mean in the dark ages?

Leader: Not exactly the dark ages but many years ago.

Tyler: I consider it the dark ages because these people didn't have power tools to make things easier. They had to use manual tools. It was a lot harder work, and it took much longer to do anything.

Leader: So, they used power, but it was their own power not electric power.

Tyler: That's right.

Leader: That reminds me of today's lesson. When we use our own might or power, we can't do much, but the power of the Holy Spirit changes everything.

Tyler: I never thought about it that way, but you're right. I have to go now. I have more work to do, and today I get to use this tool. (Shows tool and tells what it does.)

(Exits)

Verse of the Day: Zechariah 4:6b (NIV) *"Not by might nor by power, but by my Spirit," says the Lord Almighty.*

Memory Verse Talk: (use Holy Spirit Power Lesson 5, slide A)

Supplies needed: basketball

Zechariah 4:6b (NIV) says, "'Not by might nor by power, but by my Spirit,'" says the Lord Almighty.

What that means is there is no way we can do anything for God that makes any difference when we try to do it on our own. The only way we can make a difference for God is if we allow the Holy Spirit to do things through us.

Remember a couple of weeks ago, when I taught the lesson about how the Holy Spirit is like a coach who plays the game through us?

Start bouncing the basketball. *If I decided I wanted to be a famous basketball player like Michael Jordon or Labron James, I could practice for years and not be as good as them. I don't have the skill or experience they do. But if I could get Labron James to step inside of me and play basketball through me, then I'd be as good a basketball player as he is.*

I can't live a Christian life or get someone saved or healed on my own. I don't have enough power or might to do anything like that on my own. But I have the Holy Spirit living inside of me. It's through His power and might that I can do miraculous things for the Kingdom of God.

Memory Verse Activity: Bouncing Verse

Supplies needed: basketball

Have the students stand in a circle. For larger groups, you can have more than one circle. Have them bounce the ball to each other. Whenever a student gets the ball, he or she has to say the next word in the memory verse and bounce the ball to another student. Do this until the verse has been said several times.

Bible Story: Walking and Leaping and Praising God

(Acts 3:1-16)

Supplies needed: none

Instruct the students to do the following, or choose a few students to stand in front and do the motions for the other students. When you say walking or walk, they are to walk two steps. When you say leaping or leap, they are to jump up and down two times. When you say praising God or praise God, they are to throw their hands in the air and shout praise the Lord. Have them practice a few times.

One day, Peter and John went to the temple to pray. In front of the gate was a man who had been lame all of his life. He didn't have anyone to provide for him, so he sat in front of the gate everyday and asked for money.

Peter told the man to look at them. The man did because he thought they were going to give him some money. Instead, Peter said, "I don't have any money, but what I do have, I'm going to give to you. In the name of Jesus, rise up and **walk.**"

The man must have been confused. Peter and John didn't have the power or might to heal him. He'd probably been to several doctors, and none of them could heal him. And these men weren't doctors. What the man didn't know was Peter and John had the Holy Spirit living inside of them. Through the Holy Spirit and in the Name of Jesus, they did have the power to heal him.

Peter and John took the man's hand and pulled him to his feet. Instantly, the man was healed. He went **walking,** *and* **leaping,** *and* **praising God** *into the temple courts. Everyone was amazed to see him up and* **walking** *around and* **leaping** *in the air.*

The people in the temple were so amazed, they surrounded Peter and John. Peter told them it wasn't by his power that He healed the man. It was by the power of the Holy Spirit and in the name of Jesus that the man was healed.

*We don't know what eventually happened to the man, but he's probably **walking**, and **leaping**, and **praising** God in Heaven right now thanks to the power of the Holy Spirit.*

Optional Song: Walking and Leaping Song

If your students enjoy being silly, have them sing the Walking and Leaping Song with motions in a silly way. Here is a link to the song on YouTube. https://youtu.be/ymUnSwFyFzM

Praise and Worship: Choose a couple of fast song and a slow song to lead children into praise and worship. It works well to talk to the children about what worship is and why it's important before you enter into this time. You can have a children's praise team, but until they understand leading praise and worship, have an adult leader or yourself be the worship leader.

Object Lessons:

1. Floating Ping Pong Balls

Supplies needed: ping pong ball, hair dryer

Show ping pong ball. *I have here a ping pong ball. This ping pong ball represents us. This ping pong ball want to float in the air, but it can't.* Demonstrate by holding the ball in the air several times and letting it drop. You could also have the students try to get it to float.

This ping pong ball doesn't have the strength or power to float in the air on its own. It needs help.

Show hair dryer. *This hair dryer represents the Holy Spirit.*

Point the nozzle of the hair dryer up. Place the ping pong ball on the nozzle of the hair dryer, and turn the hair dryer on. The air from the hair dryer should keep the ping pong ball in the air.

The ping pong ball needs the power of the hair dryer to make it float just as we need the power of the Holy Spirit.

2. The Name of Jesus (Use Holy Spirit Power Lesson 5, slide B)

Supplies needed: 2 name tags, marker

Preparation: Using a marker, write your name on one name tag. Write Jesus Christ on the other name tag.

The Holy Spirit wants to operate through you to heal people and do miracles, but you can't do it in your own power. You can pray for someone to be healed by your own power and name and nothing will happen. Place your name badge on your shirt. *If I tried to heal someone using my own name and power, I might as well save my breath. I don't have the might or power to do miracles.*

Place Jesus Christ name badge over your name badge. *When the Holy Spirit works through me in the name of Jesus Christ, it is different.*

Show slide B. Mark 16:17-18 (NIV) says, *"And these signs will accompany those who believe: In my name they will drive out demons; they will speak in new tongues; they will pick up snakes with their hands; and when they drink deadly poison, it will not hurt them at all; they will place their hands on sick people, and they will get well."*

When the Holy Spirit works through me in the name of Jesus Christ, then I have Holy Spirit power to drive out demons in the name of Jesus Christ. I can speak in tongues in the name of Jesus Christ. If I encounter a snake or poison, the Holy Spirit gives me the power to declare it won't hurt me in the name of Jesus Christ. And if I lay my hands on sick people in the name of Jesus Christ and tell them to be healed, they will get well.

I can do nothing on my own, but in the name of Jesus Christ, through the power of the Holy Spirit, I can do the miraculous.

So, what happens if it doesn't work. That's not on me. It is the name of Jesus Christ through the power of the Holy Spirit. It is not me. God wants me to speak in the name of Jesus Christ. It's up to Him what happens next. I don't have the power to make anything happen on my own.

Optional Object Lesson: The Oil (Use Holy Spirit Power Lesson 5, slide C)

Supplies needed: Olive oil or essential oil

Mark 6:13 talks about the disciples. It says, "And they were casting out many demons and were anointing with oil many sick people and healing them."

Have you ever seen someone prayed for when the pastor or whoever is praying anoints that person with oil? Allow students to answer. Usually, the person praying will place a little olive oil and essential oil on someone's forehead and then place their hand gently on the person head. If the person praying is praying for something specific, he will usually make his request. If not, he might say something like, "More Lord," or "Touch them, Lord."

There is no power in the oil, but the oil is a symbol of the Holy Spirit. It's a way of saying the Holy Spirit is doing the work, not us.

I'm going to demonstrate to show you how this works. Ask for a volunteer. Ask God to move on the student you choose. Make sure to have a catcher behind the student. Place a dab of oil on your finger and place it on the student's forehead. Place your hand gently on the person's head. Pray in tongues or say something like, "In the Name of Jesus," or "More, Lord." Wait, and leave your hand on the student's head. Don't try to make something happen. This is up to the Holy Spirit. Wait on Him. If God moves, talk about what happened. If He doesn't, go on without comment.

I just demonstrated how you can pray for someone else using anointing oil. If you don't have oil, don't worry about it. There's nothing special about the oil. We use it because Scripture tells up it represents the Holy Spirit.

Did you know that you can pray for yourself by laying hands on your head and anointing yourself with oil?

You can anoint your head with oil before you go to bed and ask the Holy Spirit for dreams and visions. You can anoint your eyelids and ask the Holy Spirit to help you see in the spirit. You can anoint your palms with oil and ask the Holy Spirit to heal you or to use you when you pray for others to be healed.

You can even anoint your room at home or your locker or desk at school and ask God to get rid of anything evil in your home or school and fill it with the Holy Spirit.

As I said before, there is nothing magical in the oil. By using oil, you are showing that you're not relying on your own power but on the power of the Holy Spirit.

Message: Power to Heal

Supplies needed: olive oil or essential oil

Preparation: Before this week's lesson, ask someone who was healed to give a testimony in Children's Church. If you have a healing testimony, you can choose yourself for this. Also let the congregation know that you are going to have your students pray for the sick. If anyone is sick and needs prayer, they should come to this week's children's church. You may need to ask your pastor to announce this, or you can go to individual people who need prayer.

Show slide B. Mark 16:17-18 (NIV) says, *"And these signs will accompany those who believe: In my name they will drive out demons; they will speak in new tongues; they will pick up snakes with their hands; and when they drink deadly poison, it will not hurt them at all; they will place their hands on sick people, and they will get well."*

It doesn't say anything about an age limit here. Any believer in Christ has the power to heal, not because of his own power, but because the Holy Spirit lives inside of him.

Have someone give a testimony of being healed.

Response Time: Healing Altar Ministry

For this time, make sure you have catchers and prayer warriors to assist you.

Invite anyone who needs healed, delivered, or needs the baptism of the Holy Spirit to come forward. Ask adults to sit in chairs so students can touch their heads when they pray for them. Also ask students who need healed or the baptism of the Holy Spirit to come forward. Ask those who need healed or delivered to stand on the right side and those who need the baptism of the Holy Spirit to stand on the left.

If you have never done anything like this before, remember this is not in your own power. Trust the Holy Spirit to show up and work the miraculous. It's not up to you. It's up to Him.

Before we do anything, we're going to spend some time worshipping. If you are baptized in the Holy Spirit worship and pray in tongues.

After a time of prayer and worship, instruct the students. *First, come and place a dab of oil on your finger. You're going to pray for these people to be healed and deliver or baptized in the Holy Spirit.*

Instruct your students to place the oil on the person's forehead, then place their hands on the person's head. If there is more than one student praying for each person, instruct them to place hands on the center of their backs. Have them command what they are praying for. For instance, "Be healed," or "Be delivered," or "Be filled." Then have the students pray these simple prayers, worship, or speak in tongues. Students can also be silent. Go through the prayer line. Give instruction when needed. Touch the students backs as they pray to add your faith and anointing to theirs.

When the prayer time is over, ask for testimonies of people who were healed, delivered, and baptized in the Holy Spirit.

Small Group Chat: Prayer Clothes

Supplies needed: square pieces of cloth or handkerchiefs, olive oil or essential oil

Do you know people who are sick and can't get to church or don't want to go to church to be prayed for? Sometimes you can pray for them at their homes, but sometimes you can pray over a piece of cloth and give them that cloth. The Holy Spirit can use those cloths to heal people.

Acts 19:11-12 (NIV) says, God did extraordinary miracles through Paul, so that even handkerchiefs and aprons that had touched him were taken to the sick, and their illnesses were cured and the evil spirits left them.

We are going to take these cloths, anoint them with oil, and pray over them. I want you each to take at least one of them home and ask God who to give the cloth to. Let that person know you prayed over the cloth.

You might want to plan a field trip for your students to a hospital or nursing home to pass out these prayer clothes and pray for the patients.

About the Author

Pastor Tamera Kraft has been a children's pastor for over thirty years. She is the director of a ministry called Revival Fire For Kids where she mentors other children's leaders, teaches workshops, and is a children's ministry consultant and children's revivalist. She is a recipient of the 2007 National Children's Leaders Association Shepherd's Cup for lifetime achievement in children's ministry.

You can find out more about Revival Fire for Kids at http://revivalfire4kids.net.

www.ingramcontent.com/pod-product-compliance
Lightning Source LLC
Chambersburg PA
CBHW081307140626
46546CB00022B/3443

9781955838122